THIS JOURNAL BELONGS TO

AND

BETWEEN
you &
me

AN INTERACTIVE JOURNAL
FOR MOTHER & DAUGHTER

Micah Lewis

New York

LARK

New York

An Imprint of Sterling Publishing Co., Inc.
122 Fifth Avenue
New York, NY 10011

ISBN 978-1-4547-1129-2

Distributed in Canada by Sterling Publishing Co., Inc.
c/o Canadian Manda Group, 664 Annette Street
Toronto, Ontario M6S 2C8, Canada
Distributed in the United Kingdom by GMC Distribution Services
Castle Place, 166 High Street, Lewes, East Sussex BN7 1XU, England
Distributed in Australia by NewSouth Books
University of New South Wales, Sydney, NSW 2052, Australia

For information about custom editions, special sales, and premium and corporate purchases, please contact Sterling Special Sales at 800-805-5489 or specialsales@sterlingpublishing.com.

Manufactured in Italy

2 4 6 8 10 9 7 5 3 1

sterlingpublishing.com/larkcrafts

Interior design by Gavin C. Motnyk
Cover and endpaper design by Igor Satanovsky
and Elizabeth Mihaltse Lindy

Image credits
Shutterstock.com: Beskova Ekaterina (graphics); Chereliss
(unicorn accessories); Creative icon styles (ribbons)

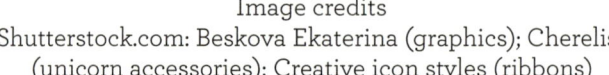

CONTENTS

INTRODUCTION

My mom has always said her favorite part of being a mama to three girls is having three best friends. That has certainly become even truer as we've grown up and started our own lives away from home. It is such a comfort to know she is just a phone call away if I yet again need her recipe for lasagna or advice on what to do with a toddler who loves to spit . . . on everything. There is something wondrous about a mother–daughter relationship that withstands the trials of life.

But how do we achieve that?

I'm a big believer in all things bonding. I have learned from experience that being intentional about creating memorable and meaningful time in our relationships, especially with kids, can be incredibly fulfilling. Being intentional can lead to great friendships, an ability to talk about anything comfortably, and an opportunity to teach and lead by example. It can help to create an environment that exudes love and support and offers a space for our children to thrive.

It sounds daunting! But it doesn't have to be. We can connect by finding small, frequent, fulfilling ways to share our lives together. Hence, this interactive journal was born.

In your hands, you hold a sounding board. These pages can provide a confidential way to communicate back and forth about all the things you and your daughter may be encountering in your lives. Being able to open up is the perfect way to increase trust and strengthen your bond. This journal will become a treasured keepsake that can always be available in any situation in the future. It will also be so much fun to fill out together in the present.

Some prompts are geared toward mother or daughter, and you'll pass this journal back and forth after you answer the questions. Many others are intended for you to complete together and compare answers side by side. You'll get to explore likes and dislikes, dreams and wishes, and favorite things. You'll peek into each other's heart on deeper levels. This journal is made to invite connection in ways that will help your sweet relationship grow. You can record precious interactions and advice, which you can reference down the road. I even get bossy at the end of each chapter by telling you to go on an outing or do an activity together. It's much easier to capture memories if you're investing time and energy in making them first. I've found that one-on-one time with my little ones has led to some of the sweetest moments we've shared together.

I hope this experience together helps you get to know each other in new ways. I hope you giggle and high-five your way through each page. I hope the prompts and activities in each chapter help you reach this important goal—a meaningful relationship with your sweet daughter.

It doesn't hurt that there are a ridiculous number of unicorns throughout this book. Everyone knows unicorns are magical beyond description. So let them make these pages come to life as you continue the journey to an amazing mother–daughter friendship that will be with you through the good times and the bad.

Thanks for taking this journaling journey together! Now, let's get capturing!

HOW TO USE THIS BOOK

One of the best parts of capturing your life together as mother and daughter is that anything goes! This journal allows as much freedom as possible to record memories that are meaningful to you both. With that in mind, here are a few guidelines to help maximize success:

1. **Go at your own pace.** This book is intentionally undated so you can enjoy it when you are both ready! Not that I'm speaking from experience or anything, but forcing a writing timeline on your kid doesn't always turn out well. Enjoy the process instead of feeling pressure to finish by a certain deadline. Together you can decide how long each person can have before passing the journal to the other one.

2. **Make it fun.** These pages are full of engaging ways to interact with each other. If you come across something that doesn't feel right, just skip it and consider returning to it later. Simply put, it's your journal. Make it work for you.

3. **Pick a color—any color.** It's fun to see your answers side by side, so consider getting different colored pens for each of you to write your answers. You'll be able to immediately see who has answered just by looking at the color. If she loves blue and you're a fan of purple, use these colors throughout the journal. There is nothing like a great writing utensil to bring out your best on paper! You might want to invest a few bucks for the pens that will capture all of these sweet memories. Don't forget to take your pens for a spin on the Pen Test Page (page 159) so you know how they will perform.

4. **Establish rules for privacy.** It's important to let this journal be a safe place where you can record answers without worry that it will fall into the wrong hands. If you choose to keep this journal between the two of you, make sure you both agree on ways to keep it protected from prying eyes.

5. **Find your icon.** Each page has an icon representing mother or daughter; it indicates who will be answering the questions on the page. If you see your unicorn, get your pen ready! Most pages involve input from both of you, so there are plenty of opportunities to contribute.

6. **Create magical moments.** At the end of each chapter, you'll find suggestions for fun activities to help you become closer during this special time in your lives. Go make memories together and then come back here to record all your fun.

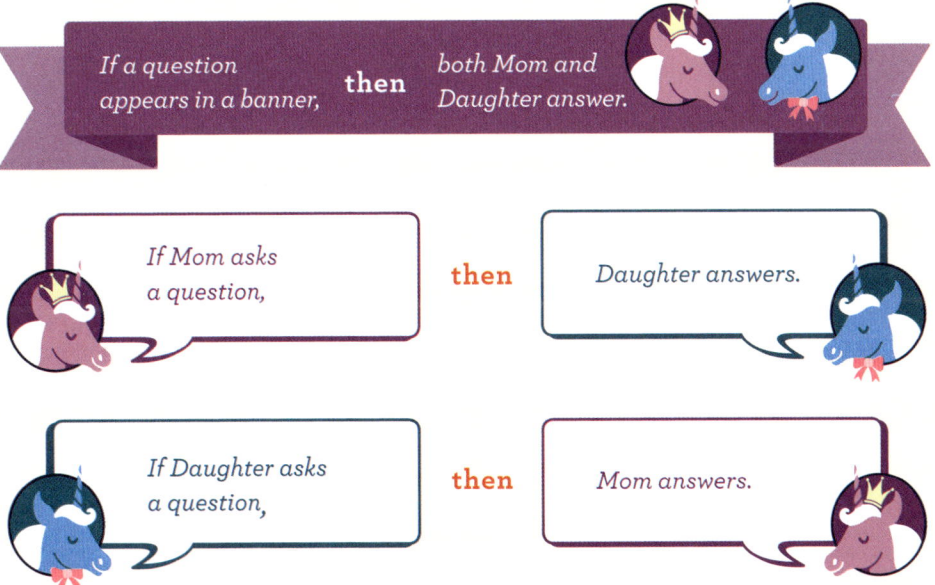

If a question appears in a banner, **then** both Mom and Daughter answer.

If Mom asks a question, **then** Daughter answers.

If Daughter asks a question, **then** Mom answers.

Here's a recent picture of us together.

Location:

Date:

ABOUT US

Name:

Current age:

Birthday:

Birthplace:

Grade:

Daughter

Name:

Current age:

Birthday:

Birthplace:

Occupation:

Mom

START DATE:

COMPLETION DATE:

AND SO IT BEGINS

It's important to know the beginnings of something before diving deeper, and exploring the times when we were younger can be a neat way to begin this journaling adventure. Here is a wonderful introduction to the times when both of us were just starting out. Get those shiny new pens ready!

START DATE:

COMPLETION DATE:

What was I like as a baby?

....
....
....
....

What were some of your first memories of us together?

....
....
....
....

What was your favorite bedtime story when you were little?

MY FAVORITE PART OF BEDTIME IS

What were some funny things
I said when I was little?

Draw a picture of when you were young.

ON A SCALE OF 1 TO 10, HOW CUTE WOULD YOU RATE YOURSELF?

1 2 3 4 5 6 7 8 9 10

1 2 3 4 5 6 7 8 9 10

What were some of your favorite playthings as a kid?

BOARD GAME

....

....

OUTDOOR GAME

....

....

TOY

....

....

PLAYGROUND EQUIPMENT

....

....

BOARD GAME

....

....

OUTDOOR GAME

....

....

TOY

....

....

PLAYGROUND EQUIPMENT

....

....

What's the best thing about being a kid?

....

....

WHAT MAKES IT SO GREAT?

....

....

DRAW A PICTURE OF YOUR FAVORITE PART.

What's the best thing about being a kid?

....

....

WHAT MAKES IT SO GREAT?

....

....

DRAW A PICTURE OF YOUR FAVORITE PART.

Draw your dream tree house.

WHAT MAKES IT SO MAGICAL?

....

....

....

Draw your dream tree house.

WHAT MAKES IT SO MAGICAL?

....

....

....

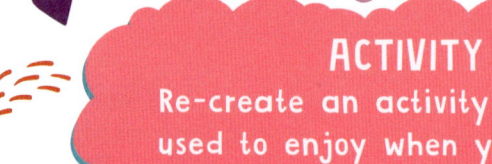

ACTIVITY TIME

Re-create an activity that one of you used to enjoy when you were younger.

WHAT DID YOU DO?

....

....

....

....

WHAT IS ANOTHER ACTIVITY THAT YOU WOULD LIKE TO RE-CREATE?

....

....

....

....

....

....

....

....

WHAT WAS YOUR FAVORITE PART?

PAST, PRESENT, AND FUTURE

Who we are today helps shape how we see the future. Here is our chance to peek into each other's inner world to understand what we think the time ahead has in store. We'll hop into time machines to visit amazing moments that came before (or after) us. Think of this chapter as a history lesson with the fun of how we view the past, present, and future! We'll explore our thoughts on everything from mythical creatures to where we see ourselves in ten years.

START DATE:

COMPLETION DATE:

When you were little, what did you want to be when you were older?

....
....
....
....

What do you want to be when you grow up?

....
....
....
....

If you could meet anyone from history, who would you pick and why?

....

....

....

DRAW A PICTURE OF WHAT YOU WOULD DO TOGETHER.

If you could meet anyone from history, who would you pick and why?

....

....

....

DRAW A PICTURE OF WHAT YOU WOULD DO TOGETHER.

If you had a time machine, what three things would you want to witness?

1. ....
2. ....
3. ....

1. ....
2. ....
3. ....

I WOULD AVOID THIS!

....
....

....
....

What will your life be like in ten years?

....
....
....

....
....
....

WHAT WILL BE THE BEST PART?

....
....

....
....

What would it be like to live with mermaids?

WHAT WOULD YOUR MERMAID FRIEND BE LIKE?

What do you think I will accomplish in life?

....

....

....

....

Do you ever imagine your future?
What is it like?

....

....

....

....

If you could do anything right now, what would it be?

What do you daydream about?

What was the best day of your life?

....

....

....

....

....

....

....

....

What was the worst day of your life?

ACTIVITY TIME
Check out a history museum together.

WHAT DID YOU SEE?

....
....
....

....
....
....

**WHAT WAS THE MOST INTERESTING
FACT THAT YOU LEARNED?**

....
....
....

....
....
....

WHAT WAS YOUR FAVORITE PART?

WHAT MAKES US MAGICAL

This chapter explores ways we express ourselves. There is ample room for emotions, frustrations, and passions to come to life. Knowing more about another person makes it easier to communicate with them.

START DATE:

COMPLETION DATE:

What are three things you love about yourself?

1. ....
2. ....
3. ....

1. ....
2. ....
3. ....

What are your favorite ways to show love and affection?

1. ....
2. ....
3. ....

1. ....
2. ....
3. ....

Describe something that gets you excited.

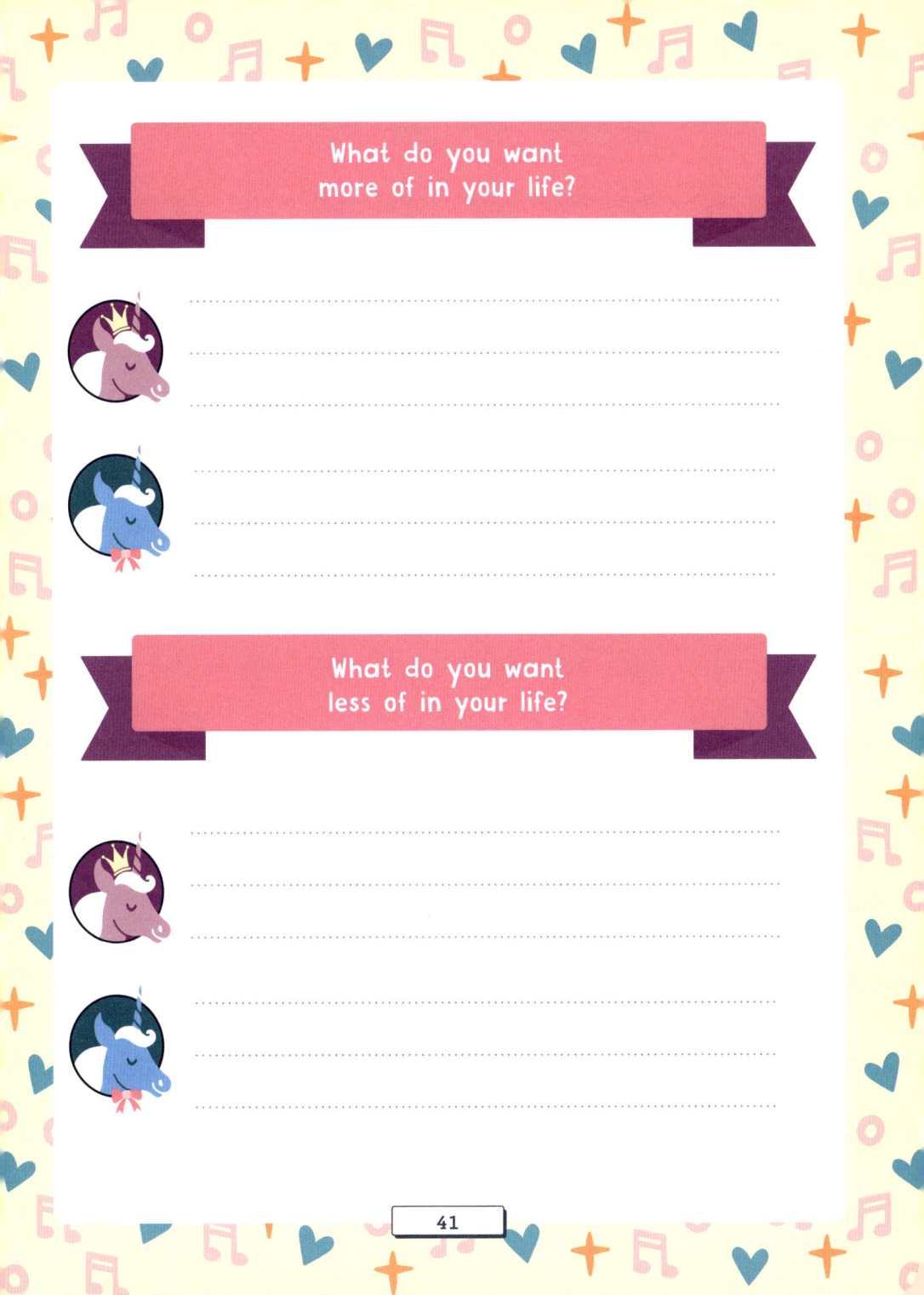

What do you want more of in your life?

What do you want less of in your life?

Safe...

Happy...

Motivated...

Frustrated..

Scared...

Sad..

Safe...

Happy...

Motivated...

Frustrated..

Scared...

Sad..

What are your biggest pet peeves?

BUT THESE TWO THINGS MAKE ME FEEL CALM:

1. ....

2. ....

1. ....

2. ....

What do you appreciate most in your life right now?

WHAT MADE YOU SMILE THIS WEEK?

Describe your three proudest moments.

1. ....

2. ....

3. ....

1. ....

2. ....

3. ....

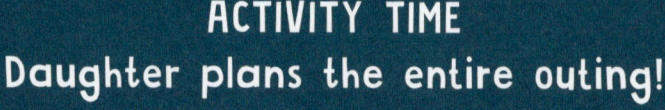

ACTIVITY TIME
Daughter plans the entire outing!

WHAT DID YOU DO?

....

....

....

....

WHAT MADE THE OUTING FUN?

....

....

....

....

....

....

....

....

WHAT WAS YOUR FAVORITE PART?

RISING TO CHALLENGES

Wouldn't it be nice if life were always glitter, sunshine, and rainbows? Sometimes, though, the best ways to grow can come from the toughest challenges. This chapter explores how we overcame challenges in the past and what we learned from mistakes and triumphs alike. We'll take an honest look at experiences that have already happened and ones that we might come across today.

START DATE:

[   ]

COMPLETION DATE:

[   ]

What is the toughest challenge in your daily life?

....

....

....

....

What is the toughest challenge with school?

....

....

....

....

What are some of your biggest fears?

What is the hardest part about being your age?

1. ....

....

2. ....

....

3. ....

1. ....

....

2. ....

....

3. ....

What is something you want to improve in your life?

WHAT WILL HELP ACCOMPLISH THIS?

Describe a time when you had to stand up for something you believed in.

What is something you really hope to accomplish in life?

What is a lesson your parents taught you?
Why do you appreciate this lesson now?

....
....
....
....

What is a lesson you've
learned and want to share?

....
....
....
....

What do you think about before you fall asleep?

1. ....
2. ....
3. ....

1. ....
2. ....
3. ....

What is your favorite inspiring quote?

What is something you learned from a recent failure?

WHAT HAPPENED? HOW DID YOU RESPOND?

What is something you learned from a recent failure?

WHAT HAPPENED? HOW DID YOU RESPOND?

What is your greatest strength?

What worries do you have about the future?

ACTIVITY TIME

Work together to beat a rock-climbing wall, master an escape room, or complete any challenging activity.

WHAT DID YOU DO?

....

....

....

....

....

WHAT WAS THE MOST CHALLENGING PART?

....

....

....

....

....

....

WHAT WAS YOUR FAVORITE PART?

A FRIEND TO THE END

We are who we are in part because of our friends. This chapter takes a peek into the friendships that mean so much to us. Let's share what we love most about our friends and what it means to be a good one. We'll also have some room to share guidance about overcoming peer pressure and other sticky situations. This is a place to step outside our own heads to really consider what being a good friend is all about.

START DATE:

COMPLETION DATE:

If you had pen pals from all over the world, what would you ask them?

1. ....

....

2. ....

....

3. ....

....

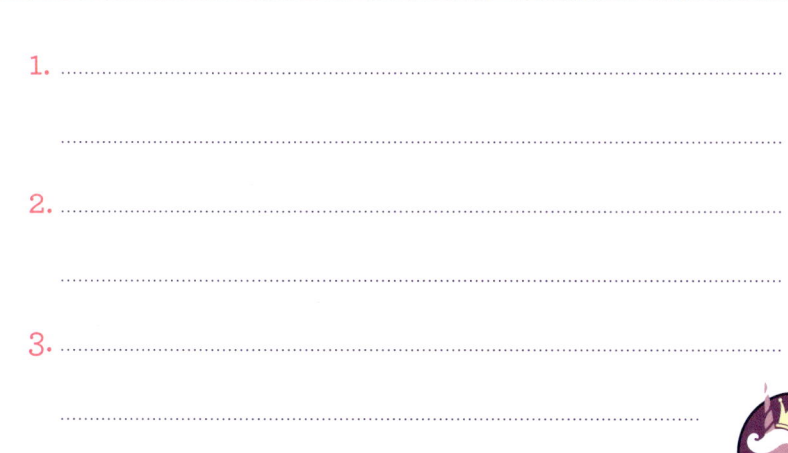

1. ....

....

2. ....

....

3. ....

....

Who is your best friend? What makes this person so great?

What are three unbreakable rules for being a friend?

1. ....
2. ....
3. ....

1. ....
2. ....
3. ....

What's the nicest thing someone ever did for you?

....
....
....

....
....
....

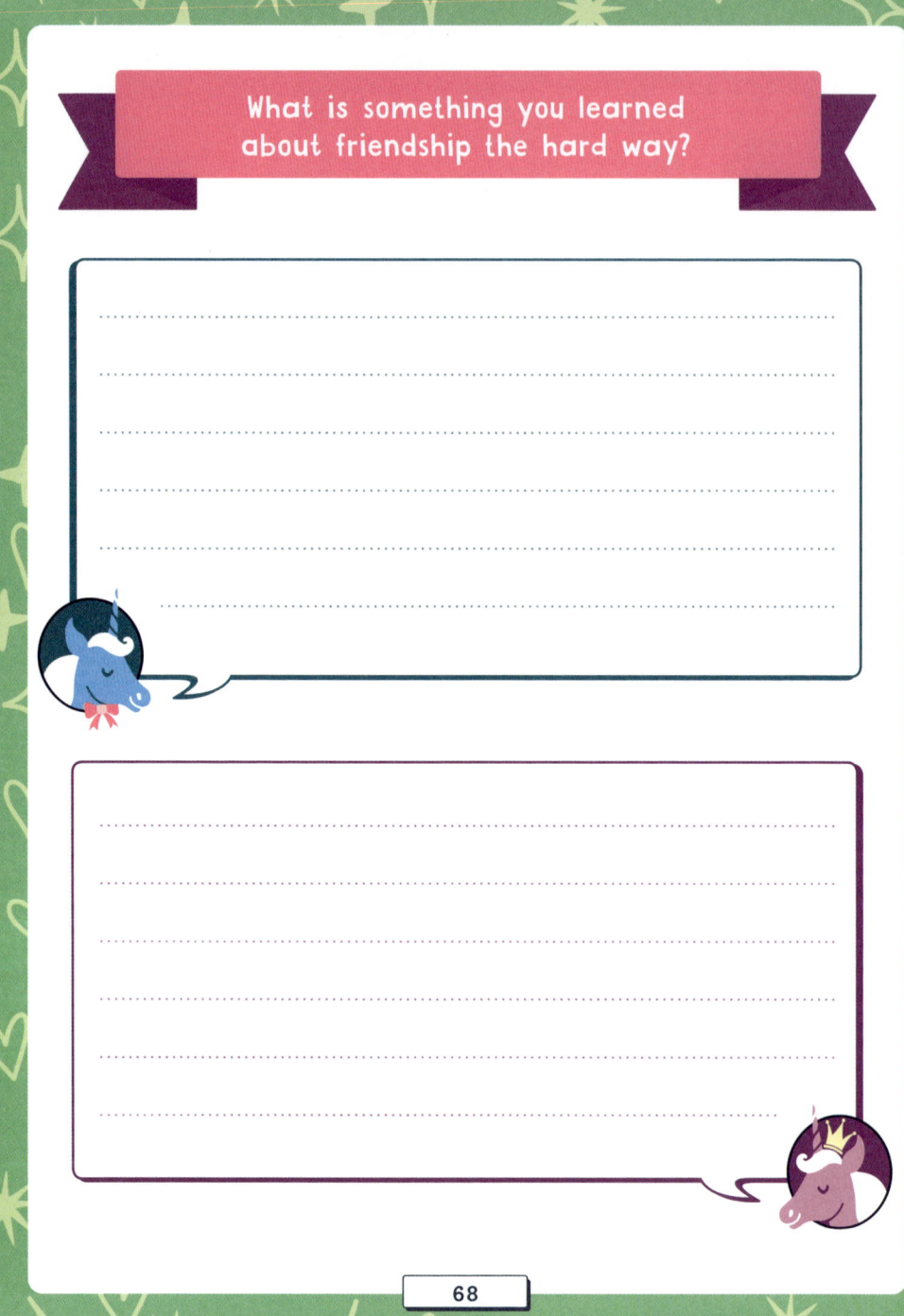

What is something you learned about friendship the hard way?

What is your favorite part about being someone's friend?

Describe a time when you had to deal with peer pressure.

....
....
....

....
....
....

WHAT DID YOU LEARN FROM IT?

....
....
....

....
....

Describe the three most important character traits in a friend.

1. ....
2. ....
   3. ....

1. ....
2. ....
3. ....

DRAW A PICTURE OF YOUR FAVORITE ACTIVITY TO DO WITH FRIENDS.

What is the first thing you notice about someone?

ACTIVITY TIME
Invite some friends over for
games and goodies.

WHAT DID YOU DO?

WHAT DID YOU EAT?

WHAT WAS YOUR FAVORITE PART?

OUR FAVORITE THINGS

XOXO

Everyone loves a chance to share her favorite anything when someone finally asks! This chapter captures those favorite things for every topic imaginable. Because food is important, it gets an appropriate spotlight in these pages. We also learn about favorite colors, books, and superheroes, just to name a few. It's good to know each other better, starting with the basics of what we love. If you're excited about lots of lists, these pages are for you.

START DATE:

COMPLETION DATE:

Describe your favorite foods.

BREAKFAST	BREAKFAST
LUNCH	LUNCH
DINNER	DINNER
SNACK	SNACK
DRINK	DRINK
DESSERT	DESSERT

What are your top three sports to play?

1. ....
2. ....
3. ....

1. ....
2. ....
3. ....

What are your top three sports to watch?

1. ....
2. ....
3. ....

1. ....
2. ....
3. ....

Who are your favorite athletes?

1. ....
2. ....
3. ....

1. ....
2. ....
3. ....

WHAT DO YOU MOST ANTICIPATE EACH YEAR?

WHAT IS YOUR FAVORITE SEASON?

SPRING

SUMMER

FALL

WINTER

Who is your favorite teacher and why?

THIS IS MY FAVORITE SCHOOL SUBJECT:

What is your favorite book?

THIS IS MY FAVORITE PART:

Movies

1..

2..

3..

TV Shows

1..

2..

3..

Games

1..

2..

3..

Celebrities

1..

2..

3..

Musical Artists

1..

2..

3..

Songs

1..

2..

3..

Movies

1..

2..

3..

TV Shows

1..

2..

3..

Games

1..

2..

3..

Celebrities

1..

2..

3..

Musical Artists

1..

2..

3..

Songs

1..

2..

3..

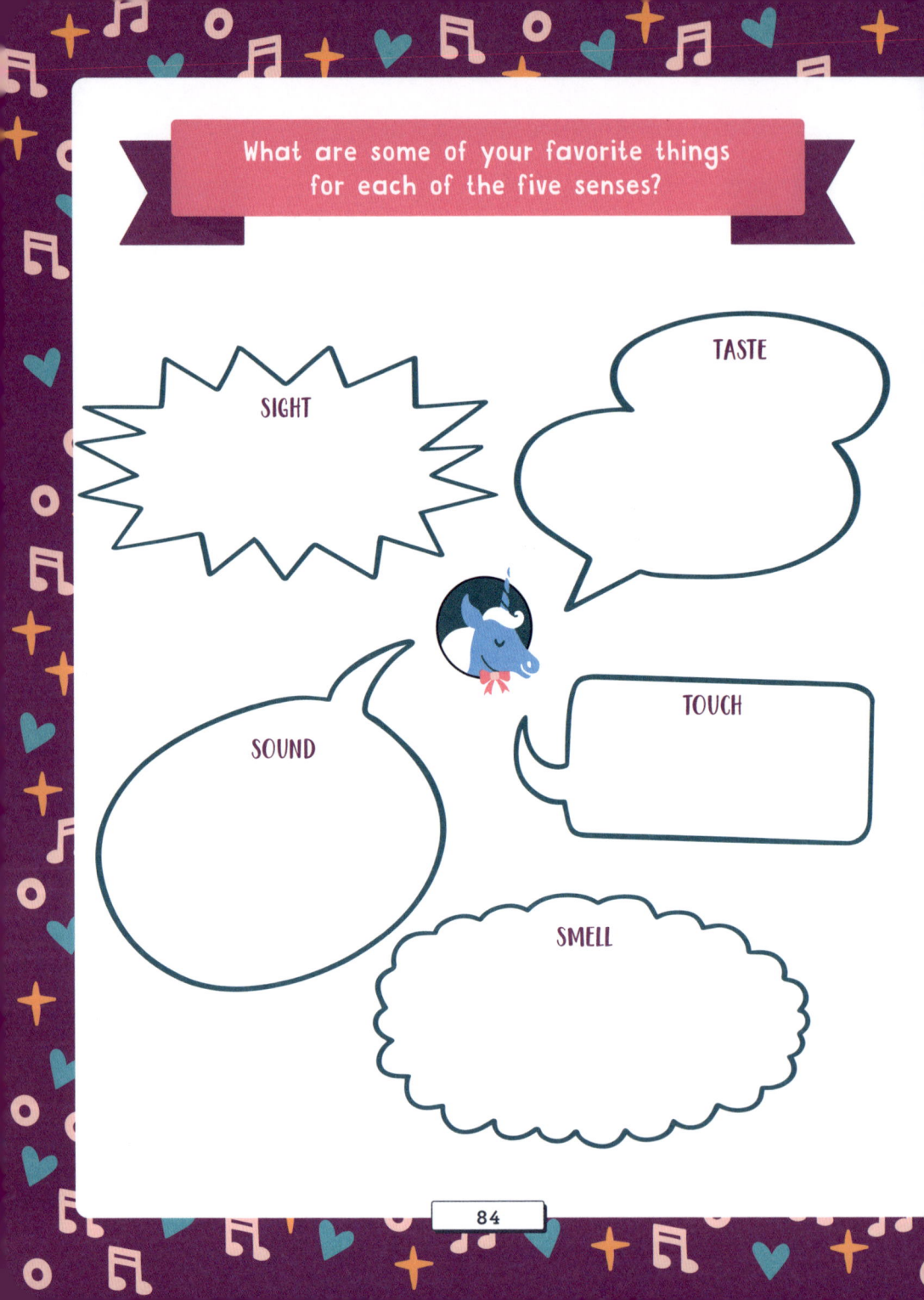

What are some of your favorite things for each of the five senses?

SIGHT

TASTE

SOUND

TOUCH

SMELL

What are some of your favorite things for each of the five senses?

SIGHT

TASTE

SOUND

TOUCH

SMELL

DRAW A PICTURE OF YOUR
FAVORITE WAY TO SPEND FREE TIME.

What are some of your other favorite things?

Favorite color...

Favorite superhero..

Favorite weather ....

Favorite animal..

Favorite article of clothing...

Favorite color...

Favorite superhero..

Favorite weather ....

Favorite animal..

Favorite article of clothing..

ACTIVITY TIME
Visit an ice cream shop and discuss
your favorite flavors.

WHERE DID YOU GO?

....

....

....

....

....

WHAT FLAVOR DID YOU CHOOSE?

WHAT WAS YOUR FAVORITE PART?

JUST BETWEEN YOU AND ME

xoxo

Knowledge is power, and when you know more about each other, you can be a force for good in each other's lives. These pages are a sweet way to reminisce about all that makes your relationship so special. We'll discover meaningful insights and find suggestions for ways to spend even more quality time together. Time often passes a little too quickly, so this chapter will let you create a snapshot of what matters most to both of you right now. We'll capture some of that magic here.

START DATE:

COMPLETION DATE:

What is your favorite part about being my mom?

....

....

....

....

What is your favorite part about being my daughter?

....

....

....

....

**What character trait of mine
do you like most?**

**What three words would
you use to describe me?**

1. ....

2. ....

3. ....

What character trait of mine
do you like most?

What three words would
you use to describe me?

1. ....

2. ....

3. ....

What do you most look forward to when you wake up each day?

....

....

....

....

....

....

WHAT DOES A HUG FEEL LIKE TO YOU?

....

....

....

....

....

WHAT DOES A HUG FEEL LIKE TO YOU?

What are some ways you like to spend time with me?

What are some ways you like to
spend time with me?

What are your favorite ways to show support for me?

....

....

....

What can I do to help encourage and support you better?

....

....

....

What do you think have been our three best adventures together?

1. ....

2. ....

3. ....

1. ....

2. ....

3. ....

BUT THIS WAS A DISASTER!

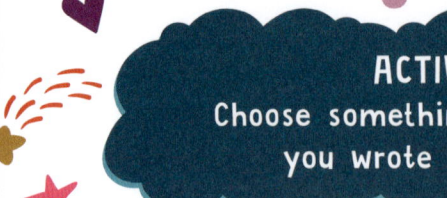

ACTIVITY TIME
Choose something from the answers
you wrote on pages 96-97.

WHAT DID YOU DO?

....
....
....

....
....
....

WHAT ACTIVITY DO YOU WANT TO DO NEXT?

....
....
....

....
....
....

WHAT WAS YOUR FAVORITE PART?

OUR HOME

Our home can be a wonderful place to spend time together. Home and the people we share it with have a huge impact on our world. These pages explore those relatives we love very much. It also opens up discussions about the space itself and how we spend time there as a family. No matter what your living situation, this is a way to help make it even better. A happy family really is what it's all about.

START DATE:

COMPLETION DATE:

Who do you admire in our family and why?

Who are your favorite relatives and why?

1. ....
....

2. ....
....

3. ....
....

WHAT IS SOMETHING THAT MAKES OUR FAMILY SPECIAL?

....
....
....
....

Who are your favorite relatives and why?

1. ....

....

2. ....

....

3. ....

....

WHAT IS SOMETHING THAT MAKES OUR FAMILY SPECIAL?

....

....

....

....

How would you spend a rainy day at home?

....

....

....

DRAW A PICTURE OF WHAT YOU WOULD DO.

How would you spend a rainy day at home?

DRAW A PICTURE OF WHAT YOU WOULD DO.

If you could have any animal as your pet, what would you choose?

....

....

....

....

WHAT WOULD YOU NAME IT?

WHERE WOULD IT SLEEP?

WHAT WOULD IT EAT?

DRAW A PICTURE OF YOUR DREAM PET HERE.

If our home caught on fire and all the people and pets were safe, what would you want to save?

What are three things that you like most about where we live?

1. ....
....

2. ....
....

3. ....
....

1. ....
....

2. ....
....

3. ....
....

Draw a picture of your dream bedroom.

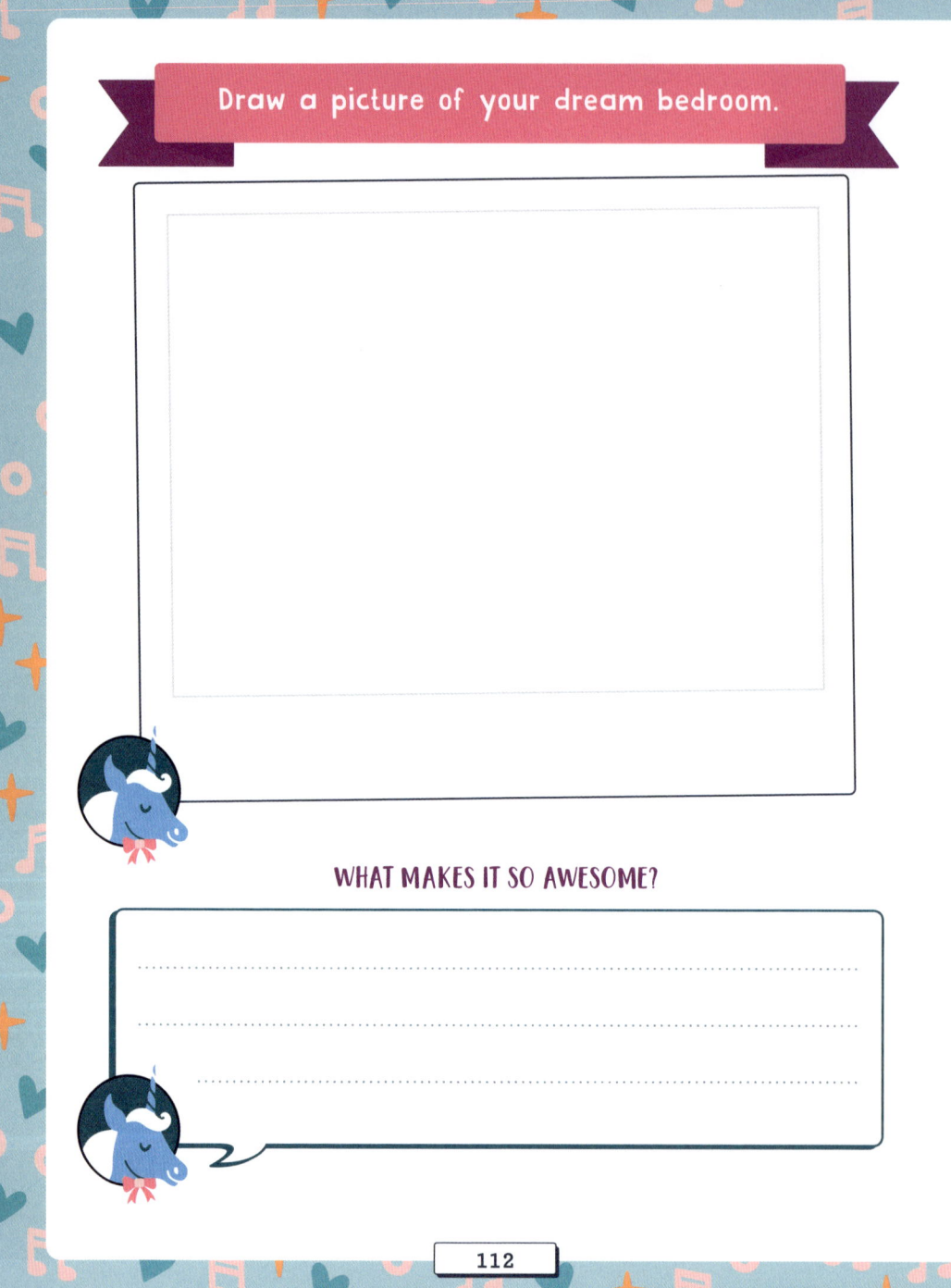

WHAT MAKES IT SO AWESOME?

Draw a picture of your dream bedroom.

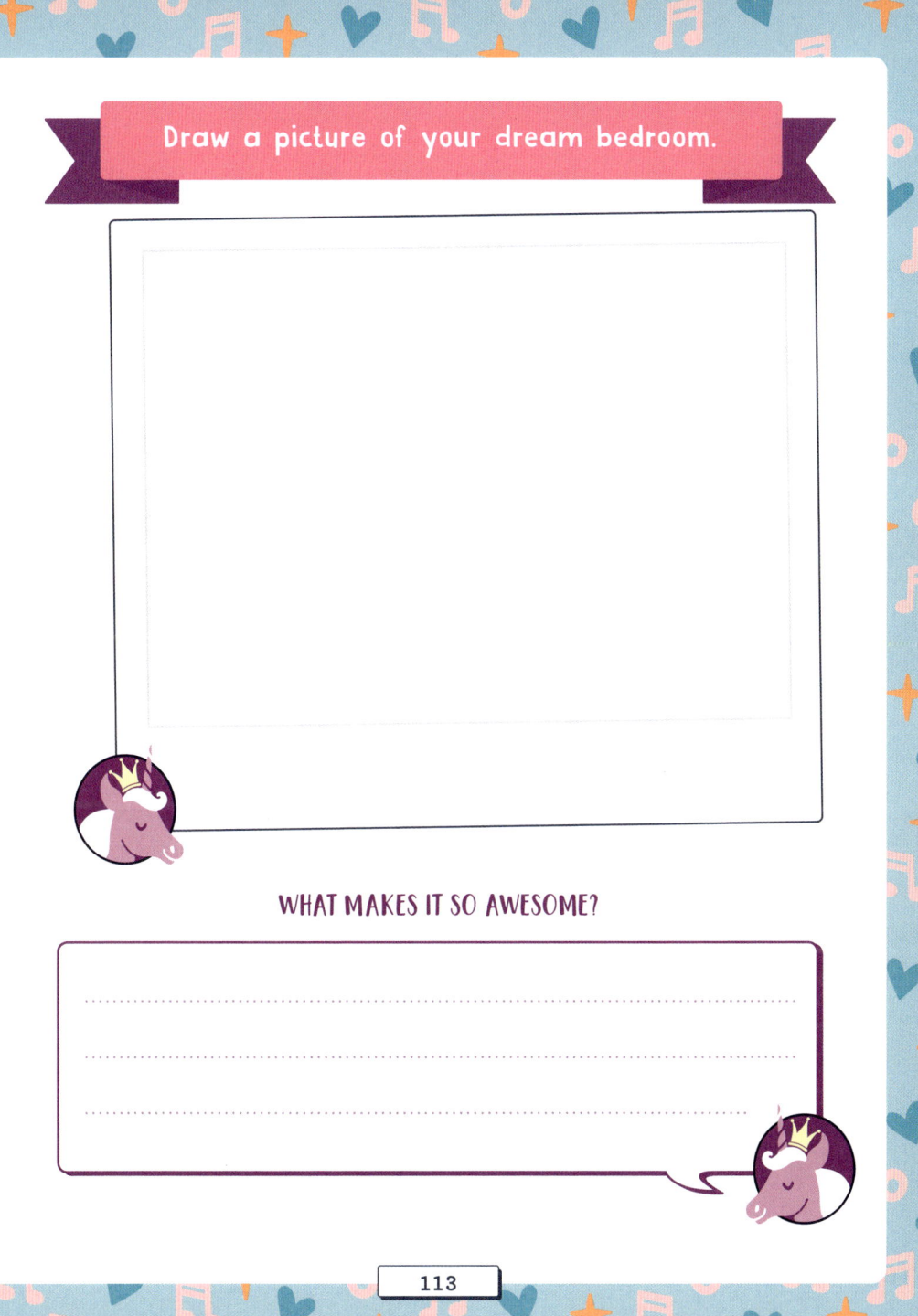

WHAT MAKES IT SO AWESOME?

You get to make all the house rules. What rules would you make?

1. ....

2. ....

3. ....

4. ....

5. ....

6. ....

7 ....

8. ....

FAVORITE CHORE:

....

LEAST FAVORITE CHORE:

....

You get to make all the house rules. What rules would you make?

1. ....

2. ....

3. ....

4. ....

5. ....

6. ....

7 ....

8. ....

FAVORITE CHORE:

....

LEAST FAVORITE CHORE:

....

ACTIVITY TIME
Build a pillow fort and eat a picnic inside it.

DRAW A BLUEPRINT OF THE PILLOW FORT.

WHAT DID YOU EAT?

....

....

....

....

WHAT WAS YOUR FAVORITE PART?

EXPLORING THE WORLD

As nice as it would be to stay in the coziness of our home forever, there is a world out there waiting to be explored. In these pages we'll record our greatest adventures and future travel aspirations. We'll learn more about how we interact with others, as well as what we want to bring with us if we're ever stranded alone on an island. Let's explore all of it!

START DATE:

COMPLETION DATE:

Describe your perfect day.

WHAT WOULD BE THE BEST PART?

If you were stranded on an island, what three things would you want with you?

1. ....
2. ....
3. ....

1. ....
2. ....
3. ....

I WOULD LOVE THIS ABOUT BEING STRANDED:

....
....
....
....

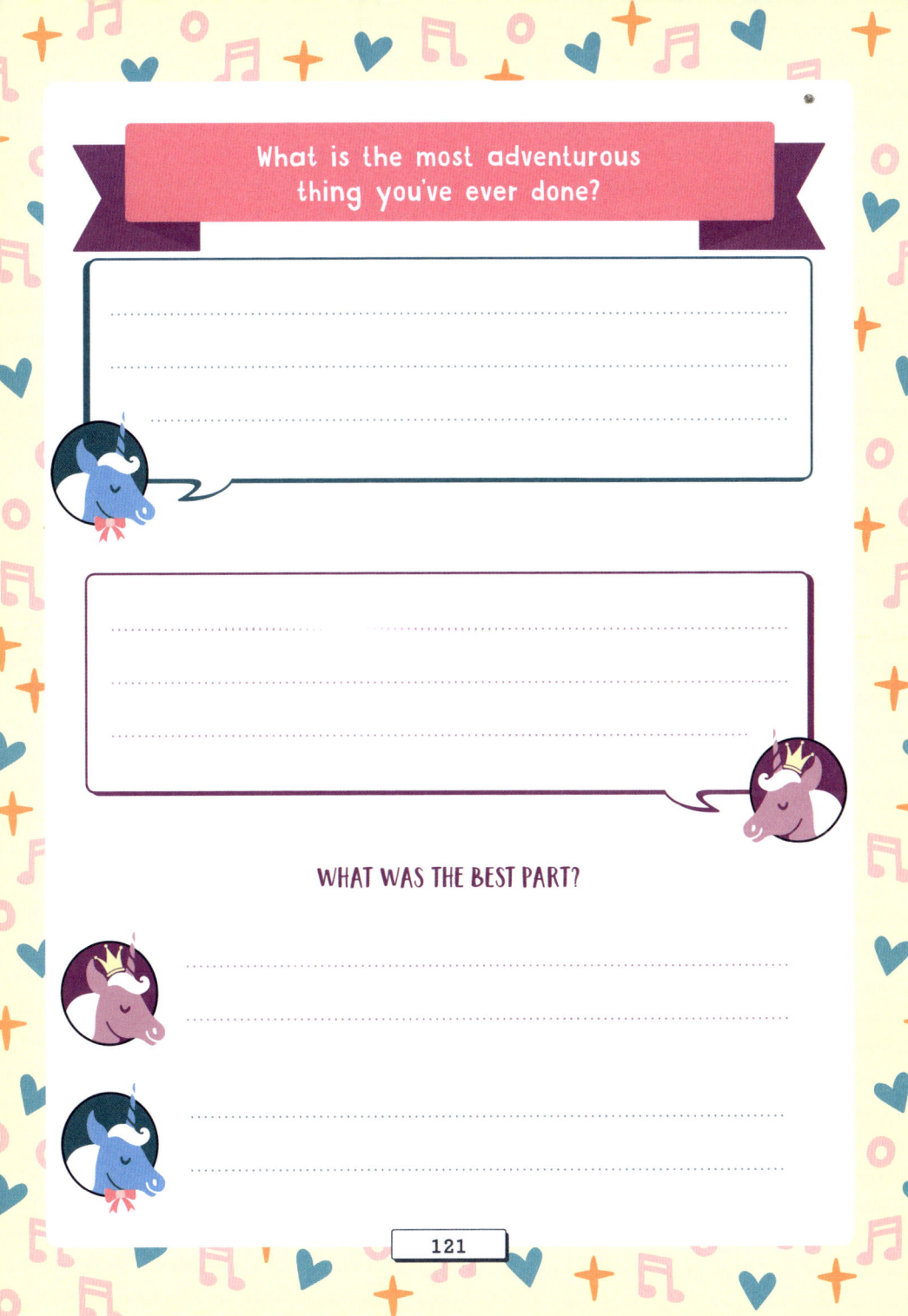

What is the most adventurous thing you've ever done?

WHAT WAS THE BEST PART?

WOULD YOU RIDE A ROLLER COASTER
THAT GOES UPSIDE DOWN?

☐ HECK YES I WOULD!

☐ NOT ON YOUR LIFE.

WOULD YOU DIVE INTO A POOL WITH SHARKS?

☐ HECK YES I WOULD!

☐ NOT ON YOUR LIFE.

WOULD YOU BUNGEE JUMP?

☐ HECK YES I WOULD!

☐ NOT ON YOUR LIFE.

WOULD YOU SKYDIVE?

☐ HECK YES I WOULD!

☐ NOT ON YOUR LIFE.

If you could live anywhere in the world, where would you choose and why?

NAME FOUR PLACES THAT YOU WANT TO VISIT.

1. ....
2. ....
3. ....
4. ....

1. ....
2. ....
3. ....
4. ....

ACTIVITY TIME
Go on a hike or a nature walk.

WHERE DID YOU GO?

WHAT WAS THE MOST INTERESTING
THING YOU SAW?

WHAT WAS YOUR FAVORITE PART?

IMAGINE THAT!

Invisibility, superpowers, and changing into animals—this chapter is right up our magical alley. We'll find new and insightful ways to learn more. Learning these lesser-known parts about ourselves can really open our eyes. And the more we know, the more we can strengthen our incredible bond.

START DATE:

COMPLETION DATE:

If you could have any superpower, what would you choose and why?

Would you want to be famous?

- [ ] HECK YES I WOULD!
- [ ] NOT ON YOUR LIFE.

WHAT WOULD YOU LIKE ABOUT IT?

WHAT WOULD BE THE HARDEST PART?

THIS WOULD MAKE ME FAMOUS:

Would you want to be famous?

☐ HECK YES I WOULD!

☐ NOT ON YOUR LIFE.

WHAT WOULD YOU LIKE ABOUT IT?

WHAT WOULD BE THE HARDEST PART?

THIS WOULD MAKE ME FAMOUS:

Who are your heroes?

....
....
....
....

DRAW OR PASTE A PICTURE OF YOUR BIGGEST HERO.

....

....

....

....

DRAW OR PASTE A PICTURE OF YOUR BIGGEST HERO.

1. ....
....
2. ....
....
3. ....
....

1. ....
....
2. ....
....
3. ....
....

If you could be invisible for a day, what would you do?

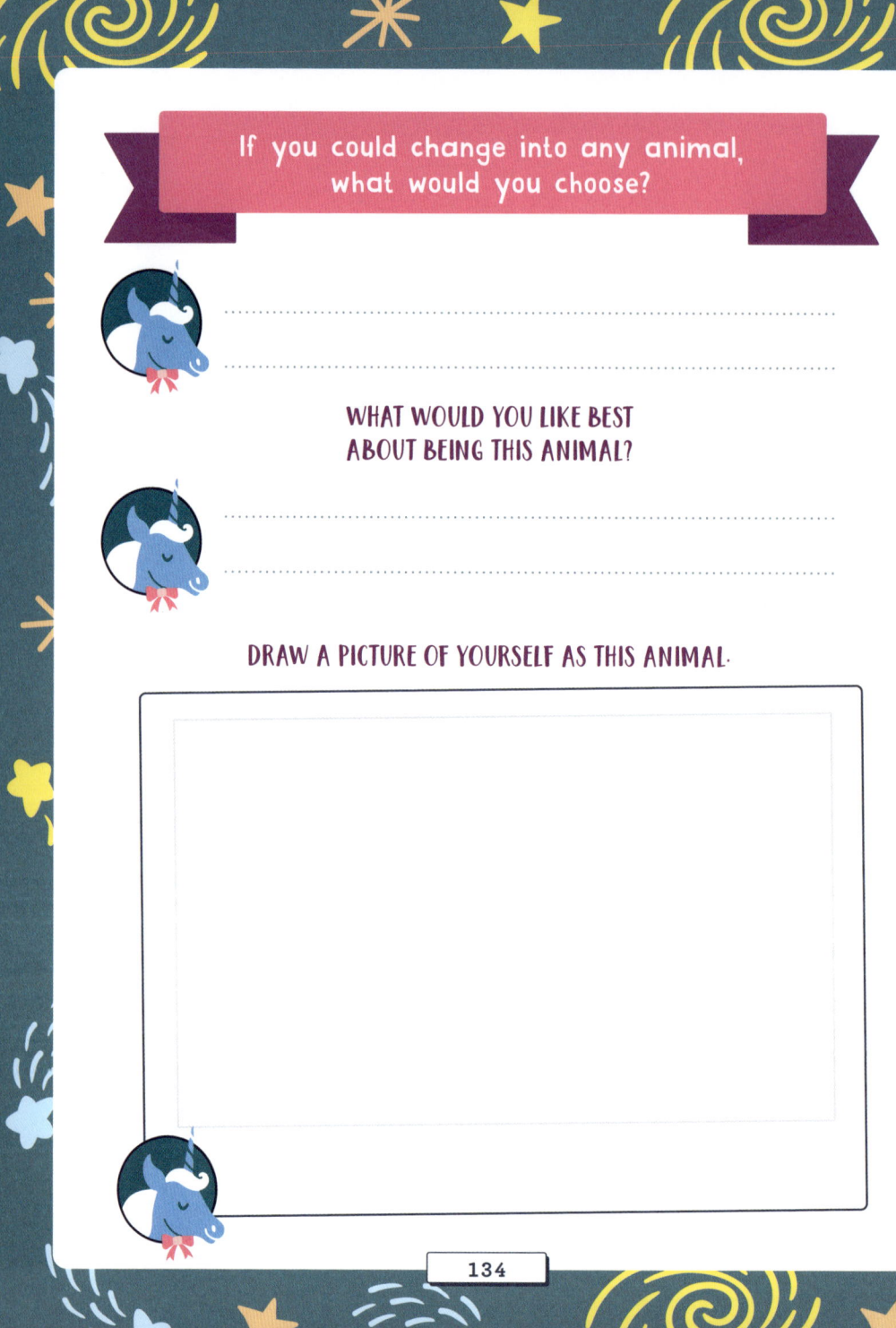

If you could change into any animal, what would you choose?

WHAT WOULD YOU LIKE BEST
ABOUT BEING THIS ANIMAL?

DRAW A PICTURE OF YOURSELF AS THIS ANIMAL.

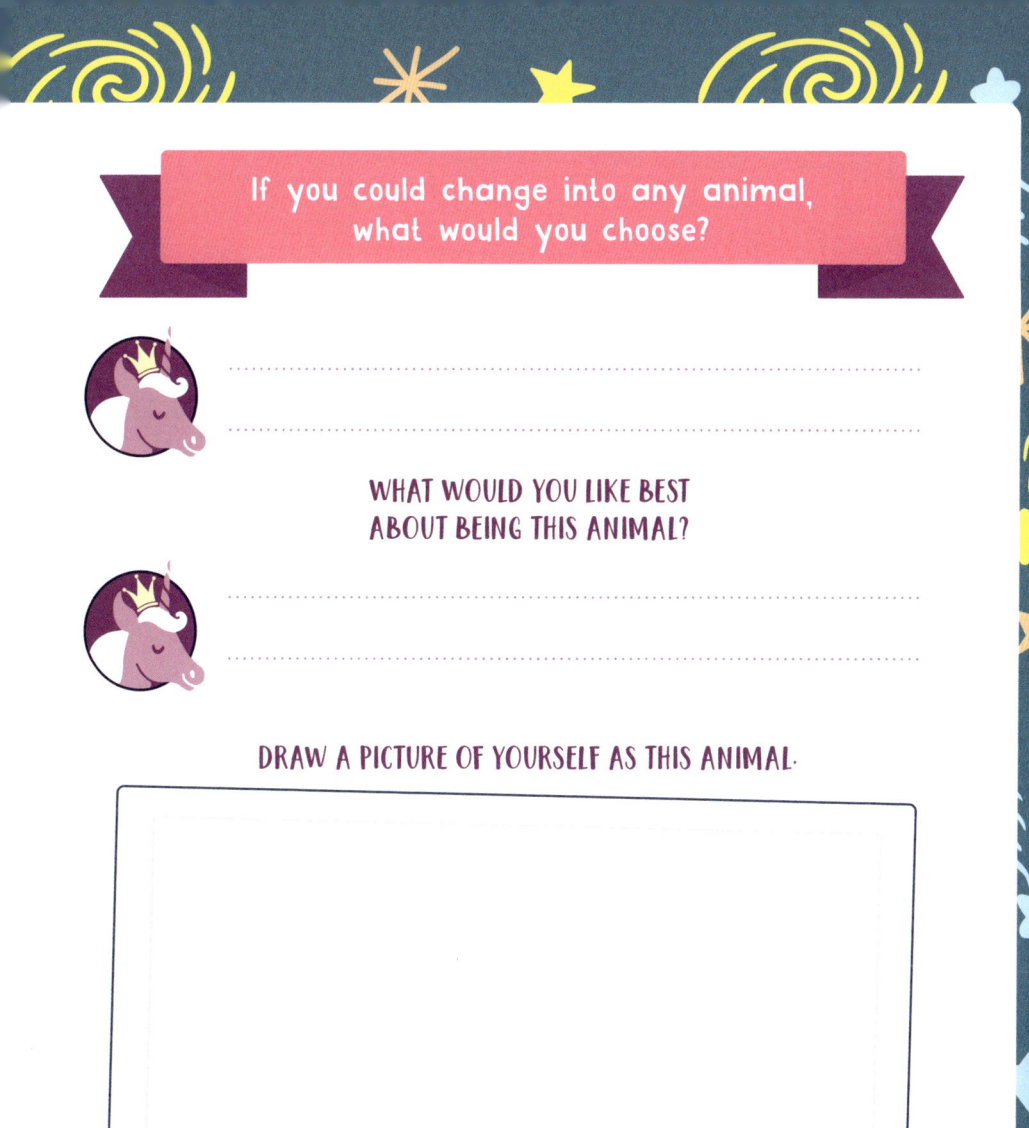

If you could change into any animal, what would you choose?

....

....

WHAT WOULD YOU LIKE BEST ABOUT BEING THIS ANIMAL?

....

....

DRAW A PICTURE OF YOURSELF AS THIS ANIMAL.

135

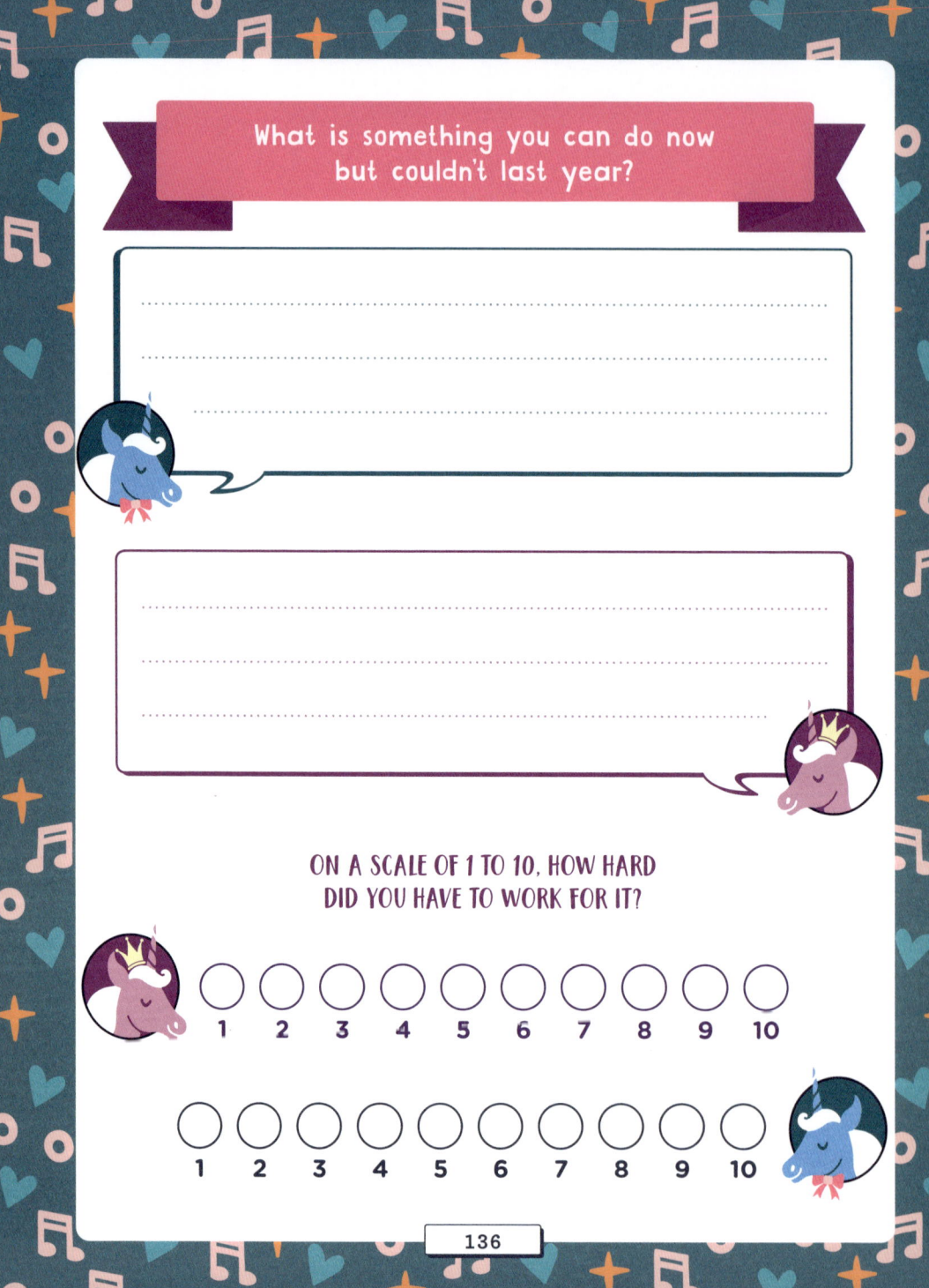

What is something you can do now but couldn't last year?

ON A SCALE OF 1 TO 10, HOW HARD DID YOU HAVE TO WORK FOR IT?

1 2 3 4 5 6 7 8 9 10

1 2 3 4 5 6 7 8 9 10

....
....
....
....
....
....
....
....

My strongest part: ....
....
....
....

My strongest part: ....
....
....
....

ACTIVITY TIME
Make snacks and watch an adventure movie.

WHAT DID YOU WATCH?

....

....

....

WHAT DID YOU EAT?

....

....

....

LIST THREE MOVIES THAT YOU WANT TO WATCH NEXT.

1. ....
2. ....
3. ....

1. ....
2. ....
3. ....

WHAT WAS YOUR FAVORITE PART?

EVERYTHING ELSE

There are those who say it's just stuff. But we can understand each other better when we recognize how our possessions operate in our daily lives. In these pages, we explore who likes having what. If you've ever wondered what the other person would do with a whole lot of money, you're about to find out. We also find ways to look outside of ourselves to know how we bring joy to others. Even our teaching skills come into the spotlight here. This chapter is a great way to discover what matters most to us.

START DATE:

COMPLETION DATE:

If you won a million dollars, what would you do with it?

What is the best gift you have ever given?

....
....
....
....

WHO DID YOU GIVE IT TO?

....
....
....
....

HOW DID THIS PERSON REACT?

....
....
....
....

What was the best gift you have ever received?

WHO GAVE IT TO YOU?

WHAT MAKES IT SO SPECIAL?

What do you think has been the greatest invention?

....

....

WHAT ARE THREE MODERN MARVELS YOU CAN'T LIVE WITHOUT?

1. ....

2. ....

3. ....

1. ....

2. ....

3. ....

DRAW A PICTURE OF SOMETHING
YOU WOULD LIKE TO INVENT.

What are your favorite things about technology?

What are your most prized possessions?

What is something you know well enough to teach others?

What skill have you always wanted to learn?

ACTIVITY TIME
Find perfect gifts for each
other at a dollar store.

WHAT DID YOU BUY EACH OTHER?

....
....

....
....

WRITE A SHORT THANK-YOU NOTE FOR YOUR GIFTS.

....
....
....
....

....
....
....
....

WHAT WAS YOUR FAVORITE PART?

FINAL THOUGHTS

As we come to the end of this journey, now is our chance to reflect on all the wonderful things we've discovered! Ideally, this has been a sweet learning experience where you've grown closer and gained even more love and respect for each other. Let's capture those thoughts in a little more detail.

START DATE:

COMPLETION DATE:

What was your favorite part of this journaling journey?

What did you learn about me that surprised you?

What would you do differently if we did this again?

On a scale of 1 to 10, how happy are you that we did this together?

1 2 3 4 5 6 7 8 9 10

1 2 3 4 5 6 7 8 9 10

How much better do you know me?

☐ A LOT BETTER!

☐ A LITTLE BETTER.

☐ ABOUT THE SAME AS BEFORE.

☐ A LOT BETTER!

☐ A LITTLE BETTER.

☐ ABOUT THE SAME AS BEFORE.

NOTES

PEN TEST PAGE

ABOUT THE AUTHOR

Micah Lewis discovered creative journaling in 2016. She is a part-time pilot who flies a corporate jet for work, and she has an online sticker shop with products that help others create spreads for their journals. In her spare time, Micah enjoys walking the paths of magical theme parks in California, playing board games with friends, hosting dinner parties, doodling in her journal, and baking ridiculous amounts of goodies to share with fellow chocolate lovers. Micah loves being a wife and stay-at-home mom and presently resides near Salt Lake City, Utah. She can be found online at myblueskydesign.com and @my_blue_sky_design.